VOCAL SELECTIONS
From

the best little whorehouse in TEXAS

THE BEST LITTLE WHOREHOUSE IN TEXAS

BOOK BY
Larry L. King & Peter Masterson

MUSIC & LYRICS BY
Carol Hall

MUSICAL NUMBERS STAGED BY
Tommy Tune
WITH

Henderson Forsythe   **Carlin Glynn**
Delores Hall

| Jay Garner | Pamela Blair | Clint Allmon | J. Frank Lucas | Susan Mansur | Joan Ellis |

And featuring the
Rio Grande Band

Costumes by
Ann Roth

Sets by
Marjorie Kellogg

Lighting by
Dennis Parichy

Musical Supervision, Direction &
Vocal Arrangements by
Robert Billig

Hair Styles by
Michael Gottfried

Associate
Choreographer
Thommie Walsh

Production
Stage Manager
Paul Phillips

DIRECTED BY
Peterson Masterson & Tommy Tune

CONTENTS

ISBN 978-0-7935-0076-5

HAL•LEONARD® CORPORATION
7777 W. BLUEMOUND RD. P.O. BOX 13819 MILWAUKEE, WI 53213

Visit Hal Leonard Online at
www.halleonard.com

CAROL HALL began her musical career at the age of twelve as a piano solo-ist for the Dallas Symphony Orchestra. She has since gone on to participate in the writing of the Emmy Award-winning television special and gold album *Free to Be You and Me*; release two albums for Elektra Records on which she sings her own material; write the title songs for the films *Death of a Gunfighter* and *Rivals*; and publish her first book *I Been There* for Doubleday. Last season Miss Hall was represented in New York at LaMama where she composed the musical *Wonderful Beast*. She also wrote the music for the Lion Theatre Company's *Love's Labours Lost*. Her Songs has been recorded by such artists as Barbra Streisand, Mabel Mercer, Harry Belafonte, Neil Diamond, Marlo Thomas and Barbara Cook among others. Miss Hall just recently created a soon-to-be-released album for "Sesame Street" which features Marilyn Sokol and the Muppets and has finished her second book for Doubleday entitled *Super-Vroomer*. She is the recipient of two 1977-1978 Drama Desk Awards for Outstanding New Musical Score and Outstanding New Musical Lyrics for *The Best Little Whorehouse in Texas*.

The Rio Grande Band

Clint Allmon

Jay Garner

Pamela Blair

Carlin Glynn

The Ladies of the Evening

The Politicians

Susan Mansur   Henderson Forsythe

Joan Ellis   Carlin Glynn

LARRY L. KING has written for the stage for the first time. King's journalism has appeared in *Atlantic Monthly*, *Harper's*, *Esquire* and many more. He currently is a contributing editor to *Texas Monthly* and *The Shanghai Review*. One of Larry L. King's five books, *Confessions of a White Racist*, was in 1971 nominated for a National Book Award. In 1972 he won the Stanley Walker Journalism Award, presented by the Texas Institute of Letters for *The Lost Frontier*. Mr. King has been a Nieman Fellow at Harvard, Ferris Visiting Professor of Journalism at Princeton, and Duke Fellow of Communications at Duke University. A native Texan who grew up working in the oil fields, Mr. King has been a newspaperman in Texas and New Mexico and last year was writer-in-residence for The Washington Star. He now lives in Manhattan where he breeds show dogs, and is at work on his second novel, *Emmerich Descending*, to be published by The Viking Press.

PETER MASTERSON recently won a Drama Desk Award for his co-direction of *Whorehouse*. A native of Texas, he got the idea to turn the story of the Chicken Ranch into a play after reading Larry L. King's article in *Playboy* four years ago. *Whorehouse* marks Mr. Masterson's first produced play. An accomplished actor, he was last seen on Broadway as Officer DiSantis in *The Poison Tree*. Previously he was featured on Broadway as Smitty in *The Great White Hope*, and created a stir in the title role of *The Trial of Lee Harvey Oswald* and appeared in *That Championship Season*. He has also appeared in Actors' Studios productions of *Blues for Mr. Charlie* on Broadway and in London, and the musical *Marathon '33*. On the screen Mr. Masterson played the male lead in the thriller *The Stepford Wives*, and had featured roles in *Man on a Swing*, *The Exorcist*, *Von Richtofen and Brown*, *Ambush Bay*, *Counterpoint* and *Tomorrow*. Among his TV credits is a featured role in *A Question of Guilt* and the docudrama *Pueblo*. He is a member of the Actors' Studio where *Whorehouse* was first produced. He has directed their productions and directed for stock, off Broadway and off-off Broadway. Mr. Masterson is a graduate of Rice University with a Bachelor of Arts degree in history.

Carlin Glynn

Henderson Forsythe

Delores Hall

Girl You're A Woman

Words and Music by CAROL HALL

10

Good Old Girl

Words and Music by CAROL HALL

good   old   girl_____
good   old   girl_____   we've been some long,
we've had some fine,

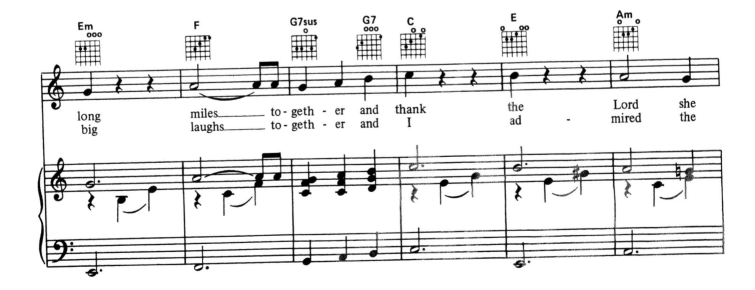

long   miles_____ to-geth-er and thank   the   Lord she
big   laughs_____ to-geth-er and I   ad - mired the

14

The Sidestep

Words and Music by CAROL HALL

Ooo_____ I love to dance the lit - tle side-step

now they see me, now they don't, I've come and gone.___ And Ooo_____ I love to

sweep a-round a wide step, cut a lit-tle swath and lead the peo-ple on.___

1,2 (ad lib.)

2. Now any
3. Now, Miss

⊕ Coda (Counter melody with chorus)

Mel - vin Thorpe has done it once a-gain, he shone his

ADDITIONAL LYRICS

Verse 3.
　　Now, Miss Mona, I don't know her, tho' I've heard the name, oh yes!
　　But of course, I've no close contact.
　　So what she is doing I can only guess
　　But, oh, Miss Mona, she's a blemish on the face of that good town.
　　I am taking certain steps here
　　Someone somewhere's gonna have to close her down.

Repeat Chorus.

Watch Dog Theme

Words and Music by CAROL HALL

Freely (Barber-shop style) Watch dog will get you

if you don't watch out. Watch dog sees and watch dog knows, watch dog keeps us on our toes.

Watch dog as-sures you that the law's the law. No ex-cep-tion to the rule,

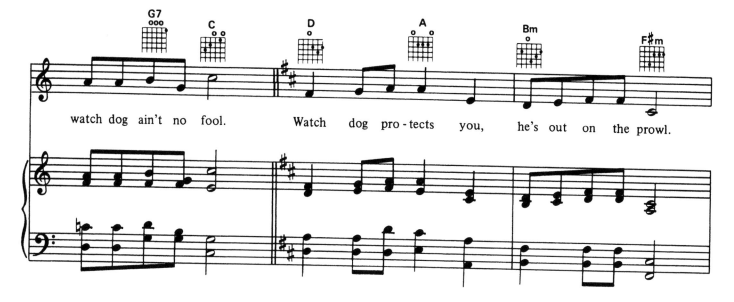

watch dog ain't no fool. Watch dog pro-tects you, he's out on the prowl.

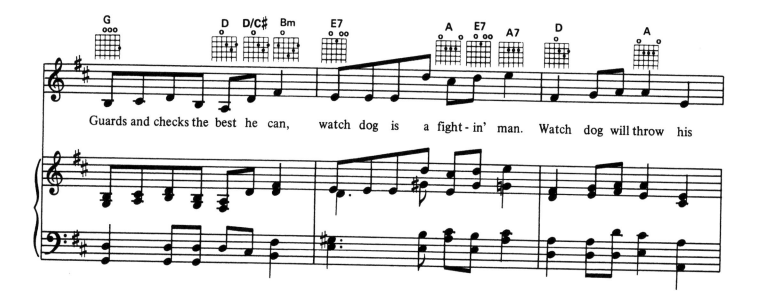

Guards and checks the best he can, watch dog is a fight-in' man. Watch dog will throw his

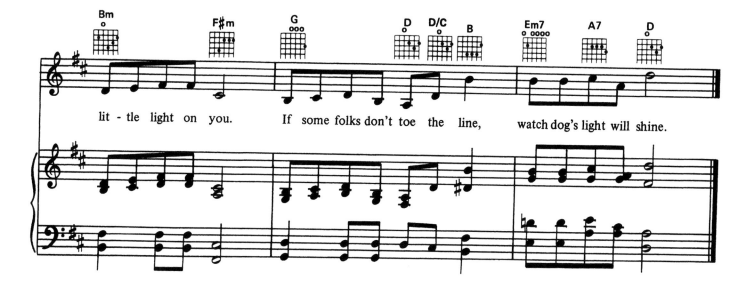

lit-tle light on you. If some folks don't toe the line, watch dog's light will shine.

Twenty Four Hours of Lovin'

Words and Music by CAROL HALL

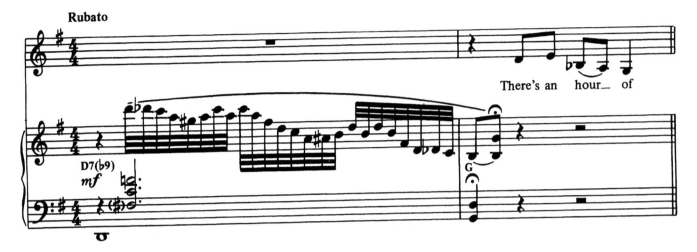

ADDITIONAL LYRICS

Verse 3.
    There's an hour of paradise
    There's an hour of Oooo, thas' nice
    There's an hour of honey, never
    Have I done this ever
    Before . . . . .
    'Cause there's an hour of gettin' hot
    And there's an hour of thas' the spot
    There's an hour of I'm in clover
    'Cause we're starting over
    Once more . . . . .
    And then it's . . . . .

Chorus

Hard Candy Christmas

Words and Music by CAROL HALL

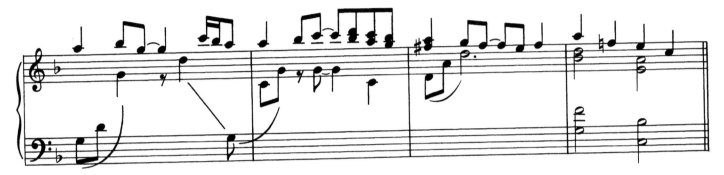

Hey / back, may-be I'll {dye / cut} my hair___ / may-be I'll sleep real late___   may-be I'll / may-be I'll

move some-where,___ may-be I'll get a car,___ may-be I'll drive so far___ they'll all lose
lose some weight,___ may-be I'll clear my junk,___ may-be I'll just get drunk on ap - ple

The Bus From Amarillo

Words and Music by CAROL HALL

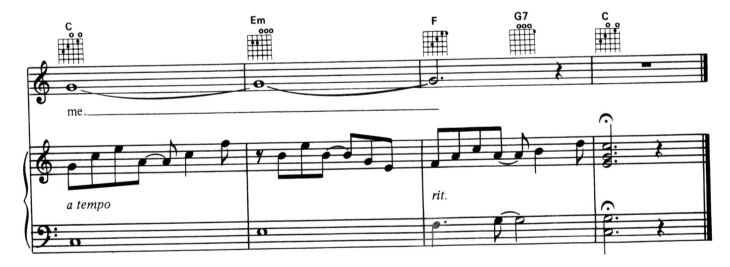

ADDITIONAL LYRICS

Verse 3.
    Well, it's hard now to determine how a plan just disappears
    How the days can turn to weeks and how the weeks can turn to years.
    And it's funny how you wait for things and want that lucky day,
    And it's funny when the bus stopped, I got off and walked away
    And the bus from Amarillo, I can hear it still go by,
    Guess I missed my only chance and now I swear I don't know why
    Guess life's a one way ticket to nowhere
    God, wish I was travelin' free
    Once I had a one way ticket to go where
    Anything was possible for me.

The Aggie Song

Words and Music by CAROL HALL

35

Doatsy Mae

Words and Music by CAROL HALL

Fred-rick of Hol-ly-wood's got these clothes in a
Some girls have cra - zy se - cret thoughts that can

mov - ie mag - a - zine_____ you send your mon - ey, you take your pick,___ you
real - ly make 'em fly_____ some girls can__ e - ven do the things they

end up like a play-boy queen.__ I want-ed to,_____ I want-ed to but I nev - er
may-be think they'd like to try.__ I want-ed to,_____ I want-ed to but I nev - er

No Lies

Words and Music by CAROL HALL

ADDITIONAL LYRICS

Verse 3.
    Were you thinkin' that you were gonna maybe have to leave this lonely town?
    Begin again? Hit one more spot?
    Were you feelin' a little like a baby who just got itself knocked down
    You say you were? I say well, so what.

Chorus 3.
    Who said life was a song for singin'?
    Who said life was such a snap?
    Who said life was a bell for ringin'?
    Not me! Not me!
    So ask me no questions
    Give me no answers
    I'll hand you no crap.

20 Fans

Words and Music by CAROL HALL

43

ADDITIONAL LYRICS

Verse 3.
When the sun would go down
In a wild blaze of light
Then the little house lay
In the stillness of night
Fireflies would flicker
And float in the gloom
While a fan was turnin'
In every room.

A Lil' Ole Bitty Pissant Country Place

Moderately bright (Country style)

Words and Music by CAROL HALL

It's just a lil' ole bit-ty piss-ant coun-try place,— noth-in' much to see. No
pid-dly squat-tin' ole time coun-try place,— noth-in' too high toned. Just

drink-in' al-lowed, we get a nice quiet crowd just as plain as it can be.— It's just a
lots of good will, and may-be one small thrill but there's

Noth-in' dir-ty go-in' on   Noth-in' dir-ty go-in' on!

Fine (last time)

(Mona) I don't hire no mar-ried girls, they're not on the ball.
Keep your lan-guage clean___ girl, keep your bed-room neat. They got homes and
Don't hang a - round the

hus - bands They're not sta-ble at all.
town ca-fe's or say "Hi" on___ the street. They don't___ un - der-stand a
And if you mind your P's and

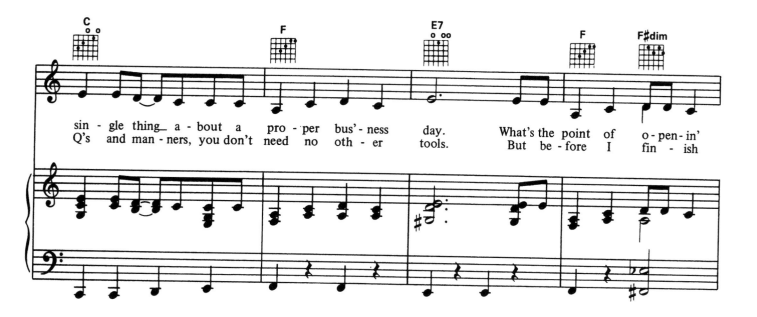

sin - gle thing___ a - bout a pro - per bus'-ness day.
Q's and man - ners, you don't need no oth - er tools. What's the point of o - pen-in'
But be - fore I fin - ish

up the store__ if you give the goods a - way. *(Instr.)*
I should add_____ my spec-ial no, no rules Miss

It's just a

Mo-na's gon - na lay it down, her spe-cial no, no rules

Tacet

Moderate "2"

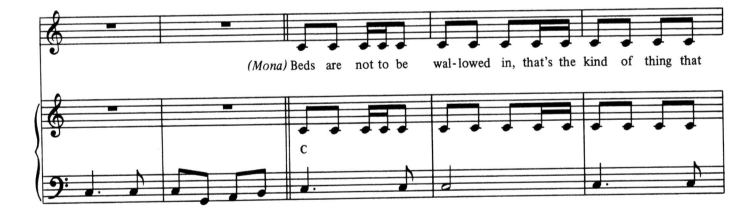

(Mona) Beds are not to be wal-lowed in, that's the kind of thing that

big fat la - zy hogs__ do, *(and it don't make mo-ney)* And I won't

Texas Has A Whorehouse In It

Words and Music by CAROL HALL

Hoedown style

Tex - as has a

whore-house in it! Lord, have mer - cy on our souls___ I'll ex - pose the facts al-though it

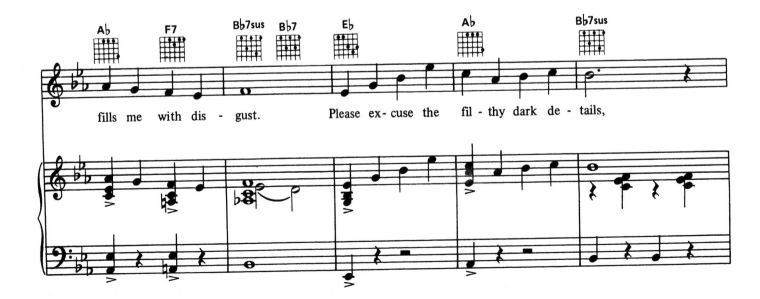

fills me with dis - gust. Please ex - cuse the fil - thy dark de - tails,

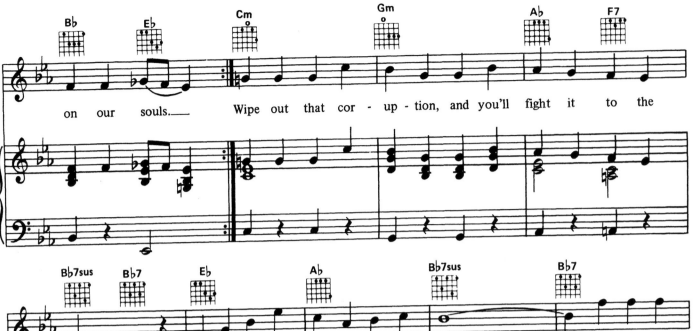
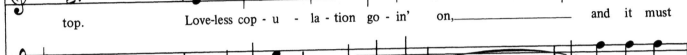